W ... nts

s

Written by
Jackie Logue

Illustrated by
Martha Hardy

D1461344

Published 2009 by A&C Black Publishers Limited
36 Soho Square, London W1D 3QY
www.acblack.com

ISBN 978-1-4081-1253-3

Text © Jackie Logue 2009
Illustrations © Martha Hardy

Printed in Malta by Gutenberg Press
This book is produced using paper that is made from wood grown in
managed, sustainable forests. It is natural, renewable and recyclable.
The logging and manufacturing processes conform to the environmental
regulations of the country of origin.

**To see our full range of titles
visit www.acblack.com**

Contents

Introduction to working with parents of children with additional needs

The Early Years Foundation Stage is a time when all babies and young children should be offered a wealth of wonderful, carefully planned opportunities to learn. All children need developmentally appropriate and easily accessible chances which enable them to play, create and imagine their way towards being independent active learners. Every child needs to become sociable and confident in their relationships with others. Parents are vital to this journey.

Parents of children with additional needs face many obstacles and will need extra support. Early years practitioners, often have daily contact with these parents and are in a unique position to make a real difference to the child in these crucial early years. A parent's experience and involvement in this key stage of their very young child's life is vital, and families with children who have additional needs must have appropriate and timely support.

Working with parents and the EYFS framework:

The aim of this book is to give support and practical tips to early years professionals working with parents of babies and very young children with additional needs.

Our goal is for every child to reach and maximise their potential.

Government evidence shows that giving parents of children with additional needs the right, timely and practical support, together with providing appropriate training for professionals, will help achieve that goal.

Giving parents appropriate support can be difficult for even the best of professionals. Some may not have come into contact with a child with additional needs before and may be unsure how to react. Getting it right can make a huge difference for all concerned.

Becoming a parent of a child with additional needs is like taking up a whole new career but without any training. There are no lessons to attend or exams to pass.

Many parents with their own unique sets of skills and experiences, may lose their identity when they have children, and this can be exacerbated when they have a youngster with additional needs.

From the beginning, parents are plunged into an alien world full of people whose professions were often previously unknown to them. It can seem like there are armies of professionals suddenly invading their lives. Many families find this overwhelming and disempowering.

But a good professional working in a genuine partnership with parents can make the tough times a lot easier and this ultimately benefits the child.

Most parents become used to telling their story again and again and quickly become experts about their child and how their disability, impairment or syndrome affects them.

They know what works best for their child and to trust someone else to look after their precious vulnerable bundle at such an early stage is a huge step. It can be very daunting for some parents to place their child in an early years setting.

By examining parents' feelings about their child's journey through the Early Years Foundation Stage (EYFS), practitioners can acknowledge and take these feelings into account, whilst meeting a child's needs.

This book has been designed to complement the principles and themes of the EYFS which covers the first 60 months of a child's life.

This is a period of rapid growth and development from baby through to an independent child ready to set off on a school career. The EYFS puts parents as partners at the heart of its focus.

This book aims to provide practitioners with the guiding principles, inspiration, and practical guidance to help and support the child and it's parents.

The Early Years Foundation Stage

The EYFS identifies four main themes to its underlying principles:

1 **A unique child**
- Child development
- Inclusive practice
- Keeping safe
- Health and well-being

3 **Enabling environments**
- Observation, assessment and planning
- Supporting every child
- The learning environment
- The wider context

2 **Positive relationships**
- Respecting each other
- Parents as partners
- Supporting learning
- Key person

4 **Learning and development**
- Play and exploration
- Active learning
- Creativity and critical thinking
- Areas of learning and development

Working with parents of children with additional needs

Parents of children with additional needs face many extra challenges which can be both life changing and heart breaking.

Children with additional needs may not reach some of the important milestones and may develop at a slower pace. It is important professionals have a good relationship with parents, especially if the child does not progress as their family would like.

It can be hard for parents to see other children achieving development goals that their child cannot reach.

Some parents seem to spend their lives telling professionals about their child's difficulties and what they can't do. It is important to celebrate their child's successes however small, giving parents the chance to share achievements and to help them enjoy their unique child.

The EYFS signals a clear expectation of settings to value and respect a diverse range of children with different needs and abilities from different backgrounds.

'The diversity of individuals and communities is valued and respected. No child or family is discriminated against.'
EYFS, Inclusive Practice

About this book

The Practice Guidance for the EYFS emphasises that early years practitioners have a key role to play in working with parents and professionals from other agencies to identify needs and provide the best learning opportunities for all children.

Parents are the keystone in this process. This book has been designed to give early years practitioners some understanding of the issues that parents face.

Many parents are frequently told, 'I don't know how you cope'. The truth is that they don't really have any choice. This book aims to give some insight into what it is really like to be the parent of a child with additional needs and give early years professionals the confidence to offer support.

This book can help you make the most of working with parents of children with additional needs. It includes lots of quotes and tips from parents.

It is divided into easy to follow sections that you can dip into and go back to at different times when faced with new situations. The content of each section is outlined below:

What's it like to be a parent of a child with additional needs?

This section gives an insight into the emotional journey parents go through when their child has additional needs. It looks at the impact it has on the whole family and how parents suddenly have to become jack-of-all-trades, dealing with numerous demands and often missing out on opportunities to have fun and enjoy their child.

Unique child

This looks at the challenge to our society to value all children equally and how early years practitioners need to focus on the child first, and the disability second. There are ideas on how to make settings appear and become more inclusive.

Starting at an early years setting

This identifies the importance of planning ahead and building up trust with the family. It examines the need to provide the right equipment, appropriate policies, health care plans and risk assessments.

Building positive relationships

This analyses what makes good relationships and looks at ways to really ensure genuine partnerships with families. It highlights the importance of two-way respect and why practitioners should treat parents as well as they would any other professional.

Bumpy times

Parents of children with additional needs will have many challenging phases when they need extra support. This section look at reasons why parents may feel under more pressure and suggests ways that practitioners can support them.

Effective communication

Without good communication there is no trust or respect and consequently no partnership. This section suggests ways to engage with parents and use their skills in your setting as well as hints to make the most of meetings.

Moving on

Moving on to school is a huge event for all families. Finding the right place for a child with additional needs can be fraught with obstacles. This section looks at ways practitioners can support parents at this challenging time.

Useful resources

This contains useful references to books and reports as well as contact details for key charities and organisations.

What are 'additional needs'?

It is estimated that there are about 570,000 children in England with additional needs, 100,000 of whom have complex needs. (Aiming High report)

Children with additional needs may have any one of the following or a combination of one or more (complex needs):

1 **Physical impairment**
2 **Learning difficulty**
3 **Sensory impairment**
4 **Communication difficulties**
5 **Interaction difficulties**
6 **Emotional/behavioural difficulties**

In addition children with more complex needs may have any one or a combination of the following difficulties:

1 **Epilepsy**
2 **Visual and hearing impairments**
3 **Eating and drinking difficulties**
4 **Movement difficulties**
5 **Speech and language difficulties**
6 **Learning difficulties**
7 **Health issues**

But whatever their additional need, children are children first and foremost who want to have fun and socialise with their peers.

Families of children with additional needs are less likely to have one or both parents in work and are more likely to suffer from family break up. *(Department for Work and Pensions (DWP) and the Office for Disability Issues research into experiences of disabled people in rates of family formation, break up, re-partnering and having children 2008).* Siblings of children with additional needs may also be more likely to suffer from emotional and behavioural problems.

Inclusion – benefits for all

For the past few years government policy has promoted good quality childcare for all children.

The government report *Aiming High for Disabled Children* identifies that many parents who want day-care for their child with additional needs cannot find affordable, accessible, local day-care.

The review also concludes that accessible childcare is vital to help parents work and to improve children's development.

It states that a lack of appropriate and timely support for children with additional needs not only affects them and their families but prevents communities from benefiting from the contribution that the youngster can make.

'Their talent will be wasted and society will lack the tolerance and understanding of diversity that inclusion and support for disabled children and their families brings.'

Key barriers to children with additional needs accessing childcare are identified and include:

1 **Lack of awareness and information**
2 **Perception and trust of services by parents**
3 **Attitudinal barrier on behalf of some providers**
4 **Lack of disability awareness training for the workforce**
5 **Perceived and real costs to providers of securing the right capacity for facilities and equipment and capability of staff**
6 **Cost of providing appropriate transport provision for children with additional needs and their families**

Government guidance

Recent government guidance and policy has identified meeting the needs of disabled children and their families as a priority area as well as promoting inclusion for all, especially by improving benchmarking of early intervention practices.

The Childcare Act 2006 places an important duty on LAs to secure sufficient childcare places for working parents and to pay particular regard to the needs of parents of children with additional needs.

The document *Every Child Matters 2003* states that every child must have the opportunity to be:

1 **Healthy**
2 **Safe**
3 **Enjoy and achieve**
4 **Make a positive contribution**
5 **Achieve economic well-being**

The Early Support government scheme **www.earlysupport.org.uk** aims to improve services for families with young disabled children. It places families at the heart of discussion and decision-making about their child.

It implements Government guidance for professionals working with disabled children and their families, published in May 2003, called *Together from the Start*.

The guidance recognises that where young children have particular additional support needs, it is important that these are identified at an early stage and that identification leads to effective early intervention and multi-agency support for children and families.

The guidance covers:

1 **Assessment of children's needs**
2 **Co-ordination of multi-agency support for families**
3 **Information and access for families**
4 **Professional knowledge and skills**
5 **How services are reviewed and developed**
6 **Partnership working across agencies and geographical boundaries**

The Early Support website **www.earlysupport.org.uk** is an excellent source of additional information and advice. Although the site is geared exclusively to children aged 0-3 years, much of the free guidance material on individual disabilities has been written by experts in their fields and encompasses a greater age range.

Early Support resource materials include a range of specialist information including developmental journals for children who have hearing or visual impairments or Downs syndrome. They enable families to track, record and celebrate their child's progress through the early years.

They facilitate joint working, by improving everyone's understanding of early childhood development and sharing information about how a young child is progressing. Where many different people are in contact with a child, they provide a shared framework of reference.

Practitioners should read these and also help parents to obtain free copies from their health visitor. There are also Early Support booklets helping parents find childcare and explore their entitlement to benefits that are all written in plain English. There are plans to make these materials available in languages other than English so check the site for developments.

Furthermore the new Ofsted inspection process (2008) also focuses on inclusion. From September 2008, tens of thousands of childcare providers have moved to using new registers; the Early Years and Childcare Registers to complement the EYFS framework, and put more emphasis on early learning.

This means that parents can be confident that all services, whether early years settings, home or group based, child minders or schools, providing for children aged from birth to the 31 August following their fifth birthday will be inspected against common standards in care and early education.

All childcare providers who deliver the EYFS will now also have to think about the learning development of all children in their care. It has been set out in a single framework, and is assessed by a single inspection process.

Early years settings need to show Ofsted how they:

1 **Provide equal opportunities for all children**
2 **Create partnerships between parents and professionals**
3 **Improve quality and consistency through a universal set of standards**
4 **Lay a secure foundation for future learning and development that is planned around the individual needs and interests of each child**

The Special Education Needs Code of Practice 2001 emphasises the importance of ensuring professionals treat parents as partners:

'Children's progress will be diminished if their parents are not seen as partners in the educational process with unique knowledge and information to impart. Professional help can seldom be wholly effective unless it builds upon parental involvement and provides reassurance that account is taken of what parents say and that their views and anxieties are treated as intrinsically important.'

Early years practitioners play a vital role in supporting parents through these crucial first years. They are in a unique position to provide key support to families by listening, respecting the needs, and involving the skills of parents.

What's it like to be a parent of a child with additional needs?

Parents first and foremost

Parents of children with additional needs are first and foremost simply parents. They come from different backgrounds, cultural settings, have different experiences and expectations and have a variety of skills.

Whatever and wherever they come from they should be valued, treated with respect, and listened to.

'When parents and practitioners work together in early years settings, the results have a positive impact on children's learning and development.'   EYFS

Shattered dreams

In the beginning all parents share similar hopes and desires. When a child is diagnosed with an additional need(s) those hopes and dreams can be shattered instantly and/or gradually chipped away through time.

Some children may be diagnosed before or soon after birth. For some it can be much later on. Many children may be described as having 'delayed development'. Some will never receive an official diagnosis.

Becoming a mum or dad is a life changing experience for anyone. We all take on new identities as a new mum or dad. For parents of children with additional needs this change is exaggerated.

They can become so absorbed with the care of their child and coping with new challenges that they may lose their own identity and some lose confidence in their skills and abilities.

'My daughter was nearly 3 before a professional asked me how I was – I was so astonished I couldn't say anything at first!'   Parent

Tips

- Try not to be judgmental
- Remember parents are people too
- Parents have their own sets of skills to offer
- Remember their name – many parents hate being called 'mum' or 'dad'
- Ask how they are – and mean it!
- Really listen to what they say about their child

The emotional journey

The best way to try and understand the parents' position is to think of one of your most painful experiences. The heart-wrenching emotions you experienced may never leave a parent of a child with additional needs.

Mixed emotions will always be bubbling away below the surface but in time parents can learn to cope and take charge and achieve a good life balance.

To reach that stage parents need the right support from not only family and friends but a good team of professionals who work together in partnership with them.

In the beginning parents may feel any or all of the emotions below:

Blame	Love	Pride
Despair	Numbness	Bitterness
Guilt	Trapped	Powerlessness
Joy	Fear	Hope
Denial	Anger	Disbelief

They may question themselves 'What did I do wrong?', 'What went wrong?' or 'Is it my fault?

Receiving a diagnosis

Parents can often vividly remember the day they were told of their child's diagnosis or when concerns were first raised. They can describe the room, the person who told them and the words spoken.

'I felt like I was plummeting down a dark bottomless tunnel and there was no safety net.'
'I couldn't believe it was happening to me.'
'I felt so guilty. I thought I was being punished.'
'I thought I would never smile or laugh again – that I could never be happy again.'

How parents are treated, especially around the time of diagnosis, or when concerns are first raised, has a huge impact. It can affect their whole outlook on life, their feelings about their child, themselves, close family and their expectations for the future.

Rollercoaster ride

How parents react can be very different. There is no wrong or right way. Some may show physical and emotional signs of shock. Some will question themselves and others, and some may go on a quest for a 'cure'.

Many will skillfully hide their inner feelings while others may openly express their struggle to find meaning and understanding.

Some feel they have to prove that they can cope. They may be enduring an inner turmoil which they cannot easily share with others in case they are judged as not coping or being a bad parent.

Some may become overprotective of their child, unable to trust others to look after him/her.

Other parents may go through an extended period of apparent denial, unable to cope or take in what they have been told. They may refuse to acknowledge any concerns. Others may strive for a cure or become determined that their child will be the best or most able child with Downs syndrome.

Assumptions

We all have had different life experiences and come with our own perceptions and assumptions. Mums and dads may absorb the information at different rates and react differently.

Not all parents will fully understand what they have been told or realise the implications. Some may feel unable to cope with practical issues. Many parents may struggle to move on or go back to work.

Alternatively, some parents may come to terms with the situation and move on quite quickly becoming very knowledgeable about their child's condition.

Many children do not receive a definitive diagnosis and parents are told simply that they have 'development delay'. This can be difficult for parents to understand because there may be no apparent cause and the prognosis may be uncertain.

'Delayed trains get there in the end. It was a long time before I realised my daughter wouldn't achieve certain milestones.'
Parent

Partners

Parents may view the news from very different perspectives which can cause major conflict and place intense strain on their relationship.

Often parents get little or no time for themselves. Statistics show that parents of children with additional needs are at a high risk of separation or divorce.

The impact of the child's condition may put more strain on one partner than the other or may mean one partner cannot return to work. Future plans may need to be revised due to financial considerations.

It can be difficult if one partner does most of the caring and is involved with the professionals. The other partner may feel left out and excluded from their child's life while the one doing the caring may become resentful.

Siblings

Having a child with additional needs affects everyone in the family. Siblings and other family members such as aunts and uncles, grandparents, etc. may go through similar feelings and reactions as the parents.

Some siblings may become resentful if too much of their parents' time is taken up with the other child.

The reaction of extended family members, siblings and close friends can sometimes put additional strain on parents.

Unmet concerns

Some parents may feel that their concerns about their child's development are not being listened to, responded to or given the proper assessment or treatment.

Tips

- Make time to listen to their concerns
- Find out what it is they want
- Signpost where the parents may get help to address their concerns – be prepared to acknowledge that there is not always an answer

Coping mechanisms

Whatever the circumstances it can be a frightening time for parents. Many will feel disempowered and out of control.

However they react, parents of children with additional needs are suddenly transported into an alien world.

For children who have complex needs it is a world of endless hospital appointments, clinics, home visits and multi-agency meetings.

'The first time an occupational therapist came to see me I didn't have a clue why she was there. To me occupation meant work and my daughter was only a year old.' Parent

It can be like living in a goldfish bowl having strangers suddenly invading their lives.

'I was lucky if I got two mornings a month free when we didn't have an appointment. On those days I didn't know what to do. All my friends were meeting up at local toddler and baby groups while I had to take my daughter to yet another appointment.' Parent

On top of that they are trying to cope with the normal emotions and adjustments all parents have to make.

'I felt very alone and had no one to talk to who would understand how I was feeling.' Parent

The early years can be a very isolating and bewildering time for parents. Watching friend's babies grow and develop 'normally' can be very painful.

Lack of sleep

The effect of having little or no sleep cannot be underestimated. All parents make do with less sleep in the first few months but having a child with additional needs can mean this becomes a long-term even life-long problem.

Tips

- Be mindful of the child's sleeping pattern
- Be patient – it is hard to take on new information and learn new things when you are sleep deprived
- Remember lack of sleep makes us all grumpy and snappy
- Written information or website addresses are invaluable – parents can look at them when it is convenient to them
- Encourage parents to seek practical support such as from the Home Start system, visit **www.home-start.org.uk**

Becoming a jack-of-all-trades

Parents of children with additional needs are asked to repeat their child's life story over and over again.

The Early Support materials are designed to help parents of children with additional needs. The website **www.earlysupport.org.uk** has a wealth of information which you could share with them.

For some children with complex needs there may be a number of different professionals involved with them. Some parents will be appointed a key worker to support them. Parents learn to become a jack-of-all-trades. But it can be an exhausting and bewildering time.

All parents have to learn to adjust to the demands of a new baby, sleepless nights, changing nappies, etc. As the child grows the issues move onto walking, talking, eating and potty training.

In addition parents of children with additional needs may have to learn many other new skills including:

- Developing an in-depth knowledge of their child's needs, diagnosis or condition
- Carrying out various physiotherapy, speech or occupational therapy programmes
- Coping with having little or no sleep
- Learning to use a variety of pieces of equipment such as tube feeding, alternative communication methods, slings and hoists.
- Juggling numerous appointments – liais with different professionals – attending many appointments
- Being prepared to have their family's privacy invaded and their parenting judged again and again
- Battling to get the right treatment, equipment or facilities for their child
- Needing to stop work or college or change to part time
- Adapting to more uncertain future regarding job or pension prospects
- Coping with negative reactions from friends, family and society in general (see Bumpy times section)
- Navigating their way around the key health and social services legislation, the benefits system and the Special Education Needs law and becoming an advocate for their child

How practitioners can help

Early years settings

Allowing relative strangers to look after their child, particularly at pre-school age requires a huge leap of faith for many parents.

Tips

- Ensure there is a welcoming atmosphere for everyone – review your SEN policy
- Have clear positive visual images of disability on display

The image shown here on the right is on the front door of Touch of Eden Nursery in Stanwick, Northamptonshire.

Scope's In the Picture project has lots of ideas about images and story books to use in your setting, visit **www.childreninthepicture.org.uk**

Time management

In amongst all this parents still need to cope with the demands of other siblings, work and home pressures. Finding the time to have fun with their child can be difficult.

'Keeping a calendar by the phone is vital. I once had three separate professionals turn up at the same time to see my daughter and she wasn't even home!'   *Parent*

Tips

- Value the child
- Always use the child's name – don't refer to them by their condition
- Do your homework about the child's needs by contacting professionals involved with the family
- Be aware of key appointments or meetings with professionals
- Offer to help parents prepare for key meetings
- Encourage parents to think through what it is they want to ask and make a list of questions
- Ask how the meeting went afterwards
- Check parents' understanding of what they have been told
- Ask the parents what they want or need?
- Do they need information about professionals involved with their child?
- Do they understand the professionals' roles?
- Encourage parents to use a diary planner to juggle appointments
- Find out how the parents would like to stay in touch – many find emails very useful as these can be accessed any time of day or night.
- Make sure parents know where they can get support. Many charities run message boards on their websites where parents can swap information. Check out **www.parentlineplus.org.uk/**

'I was advised to take a week off from all the appointments by a well meaning experienced professional. At the time I was horrified – not wanting to waste a week of therapy and appointments. I now realise how important it is to have quality family times and a complete rest from the medical bits.'   *Parent*

Journey to acceptance

Research has shown that how parents are treated and supported, especially around the time of diagnosis, can have a profound effect on their eventual learning to accept and enjoy bringing up their child.

Many parents go through a grieving process and mourn the loss of the child that might have been. Some come through this very quickly, others can take years or may never come to terms with it.

Some parents feel very guilty and imagine that it is somehow their fault. They lose sight of the wonderful youngster they have amid the maze of hospital appointments and visiting professionals. Sharing special times with their child can be difficult.

Many parents feel overwhelmed with their situation. The path to acceptance comes with information and empowerment and focusing on the positives.

In time most parents will accept their situation, warts and all, developing their own coping mechanisms and strategies.

Parents need to feel in control by being fully informed, treated with respect and being dealt with honestly.

Tips

- Appoint a key worker(s) for each child
- Empower parents - make sure parents have all the information they want about their child's syndrome or condition - **www.contactafamily.org.uk** can be a good place to start for information
- Check parent's understanding of a child's condition – don't assume anything
- Make time for parents – understand they may need time to explain themselves
- Respect cultural differences
- Be aware of the impact of language used
- Keep parents informed of support groups in your local area
- Be father friendly – if you can't hold meetings when dads or working parents are available arrange to call them with a summary and give them the chance to ask questions
- Be flexible when making appointments for meetings
- Understand family dynamics
- Don't forget siblings – hold events they can join in too
- Ensure there is a good network of support for professionals who may need to visit children at your setting
- Show parents how to have fun with their youngster – organise a 'parents come to nursery' morning

Empathy not sympathy

It is really important to show empathy **not** sympathy to parents.

Tips

- Don't be tempted to say 'I know how you feel' – you don't
- Avoid saying things like 'I don't know how you cope' – the reality is most parents don't necessarily feel like they are coping. They don't have a choice but in time learn to make the best of it.
- Take all concerns seriously however trivial they may seem to you - they may be huge to the parent

Many parents continue to experience a rollercoaster ride of emotions and there's no getting off the ride even if you're feeling queasy.

The highs can be fantastic but short-lived and the lows depressing and seemingly never-ending.

Parent who may appear to be coping one day may not be so together the next time you see them.

However with the right support parents should eventually go through a period of transition. They let go of what might have been, and enjoy a more balanced life-style by developing their own coping strategies.

Brag factor

Helping parents to see the positives about their child (however small) can make the rollercoaster ride run more smoothly.

All parents naturally like to share their child's achievements especially when they first walk, talk, etc.

Parents of children with additional needs can miss out on being able to 'brag' about their child. They will notice the smallest changes in their child and need opportunities to share something positive about them.

'My son has the best eyes and eyelashes in the whole school!'   *Parent*

Make time to really listen to what they are saying. Share in the parent's delight. If the child has gorgeous smile – comment on it.

All parents want to hear that their child is doing well. It is important to tell parents about the little things, for instance:

'Johnny listened really well at story time today.'

'Cory held onto his spoon for a count of ten.'

'Jake was very patient handing out the drinks.'

Read more about this in Bumpy times.

Parents need to be heard, and to have their views respected and acknowledged. Practitioners who empathetically try to understand what it is like to be a parent of a child with additional needs can provide a really vital support for them and have a positive impact on the family.

'The first time I was asked what my daughter could do (as opposed to what she couldn't) I was speechless and couldn't answer for 15 minutes. She waited patiently while I thought of positive things to say. This really helped me appreciate what she could do.'

Tips

- Be encouraging and talk about the things a child can do, not always focusing on what they can't do

Unique child

We are all unique. Our individuality is a strength and we all have our own share of weaknesses. None of us are perfect – at different times of life we may have additional needs such as hearing loss or the need to wear glasses.

Children with additional needs are no different. They are simply children first and foremost. They have a right to be valued the same as any other youngster.

They like to have fun, be cheeky, show off and be naughty at times. They want to feel valued, included in society, supported by positive adult role models and play with their peers in a safe environment.

Just like other children, youngsters with additional needs need to be shown respect, have choices, and be given opportunities to communicate in whatever way they can. They need to learn about our world, be helped to learn at their own pace and allowed to make mistakes along the way. They also need boundaries and to be helped with positive behaviour management strategies.

Creating a sense of fun

Some children with complex needs may have twenty five or more professionals involved in their care which can become very stressful for parents, practitioners, the child and their siblings.

Endless clinic appointments, therapy sessions and fittings for various bits of equipment they may not want to wear or use, is a difficult challenge for most children.

Some children with additional needs may be assigned special programmes such as physiotherapy, occupational therapy and speech therapy to try and enhance their skills. All the sessions have to be dovetailed in around medical appointments, etc. Often the biggest thing youngsters with additional needs miss out on is fun! Somehow lost in the middle of everything is a young child.

Play is a child's joy and a form of work. All children should have the right to share laughter, play games and interact with their peers.

A lot can be learnt by listening to adults with additional needs reflecting on their own childhood experiences. Many recall feeling like a guinea pig being ferried around to various appointments, being constantly assessed and asked to do things over and over again.

They talk of endless tick boxes which they always had to complete. Children with additional needs have a right to be awkward, tired, non-cooperative, etc. They are not robots who can perform on demand.

It can be exhausting for everyone and children with additional needs may tire easily.

Indeed children with more complex needs may not sleep well which can make them feel irritable and easily frustrated.

Their relationship with their parents is vital. How their family treats them makes a big difference to the child's well being. Children who are treated as a child first and someone with additional needs second feel less excluded from society.

- Help parents to see the child first, disability second
- Encourage parents to talk about their child's personality
- Appoint key worker/person for the child and whole family
- Celebrate the positives – however small

To be able to really support the child and his/her family it is worth asking yourself some really hard questions:

Does society value all children equally? Do you value all children equally?

Look at this image. What is the first thing you see? Identify three things you can see about the image. Are they positive thoughts? Do you feel comfortable with what you think?

Now look at this next image. What is the first thing that strikes you? You need to be very honest with yourself. Identify three things which strike you about this image. Are they still positive reactions?

Do you feel empathy or sympathy for the mum and child? Would you be comfortable in engaging with the child and/or the mum?

The first thing that hits you is probably the wheelchair. Does this conjure up positive feelings or does it raise uncomfortable perceptions and assumptions about disability?

What about the relationship between the mum and child? What do you think about that?

Look closer and you will realise it is the same little girl in both pictures. She was about four when the photograph was taken.

It is a little girl who loves her dolls, her swing, swimming and chocolate. The second picture shows she has a disability but that doesn't stop her enjoying life, playing with her dolls, going on her swing, swimming and eating chocolate.

Early years professionals need to be able to look at the second image and see the child pictured in the first. See the child first and foremost, don't let your perceptions and assumptions cloud your opinion.

Government guidance is very clear – we should cherish and include everyone and we should value diversity. The Downs Syndrome Association website has lots of practical advice and information at **www.downs-syndrome.org.uk/resources.html** as does Contact a Family website **www.cafamily.org.uk** and **www.scope.org.uk**.

When a child has quite complex medical needs it can be difficult to see beyond their health needs and remember the child within. They may be on medication, for example a child with epilepsy may take medication which affects their alertness and behaviour.

It is quite natural to be nervous or concerned about supporting a child with additional needs. It may require extra patience, time and planning but above all try to see the child first and the disability second.

Tips

- Value the child
  - Always use their name
  - Never refer to the child by their condition
  - Give them choices (see Effective communication)
  - Ensure you include them in everything
- Be prepared
  - Gather information about the child
  - Get to know their likes/dislikes
  - Read up about their condition. Contacting a family website is a good place to start **www.cafamily.org.uk**
  - Understand how their condition affects them, e.g. prone to tiredness or behavioural difficulties
  - Seek expert advice if needed
  - Be aware of any health care plans (see Including Me – Council for Disabled Children) **www.ncb.org.ujk/cdc**
- Treat the child as you would any other
  - All children need lots of praise
  - All children need to learn boundaries

Make time to hear parents' social stories about their child. This not only cements the professional/parent partnership, it helps families to see their child rather than their disability.

Tips

- Find out about the child, not just their disability, additional needs or syndrome
- What do they like to do?
- Engage with the child by learning how the child communicates and their level of understanding?
- Make a communication passport (see below)

Communication passports

Communication passports or 'All about Me books' can help all the professionals involved to get to know their children quickly.

Passports can come in a variety of sizes and styles. They can be computer generated or handmade. They can be made for anyone with a communication difficulty of any age and ability. They should go everywhere with the child.

They are important because they value the child and give them a voice. They also provide the child with some control to tell practitioners about their needs. They can also be useful by providing simple problem solving to help the child, as well as helping newcomers to quickly understand the child's needs. This is particularly important if a child has a dual placement with both a childminder and a nursery.

Tips

- You may be able to start with information from the Early Support Family File if that is being used **www.earlysupport.org.uk**
- All children could have passports so as not to single out youngsters with additional needs
- Passports need to be positive and reflect their personality
- Passports need to encourage interaction from the child

For instance:

At Daniel's nursery all the children have passports. On the front page of Daniel's passport it says 'I can sign the words car, ball and cat. Can you?'

They can also be a really useful tool to help parents bond with their child and to pass on useful information to your setting.

Tips

- Try to hold 'Come and make a passport' mornings for parents
- Encourage children to draw, paint pictures or stick photographs and items of interest into the passport
- The book is owned by the child
- It is about their personality, their likes and dislikes
- It is not an extension of the red health check book but may include crucial health information to enable people to look after the child safely
- It can be used as a useful guide when the child starts a new setting/school but it needs to be reviewed and updated regularly

For further information and passport templates visit **www.scope.org.uk** or **www.callcentrescotland.org.uk**

Benefits for everyone

It is important to recognise that including children with additional needs in your setting is not a one-sided arrangement. It does not just benefit the child but everyone else involved.

Friendships and relationships are an essential part of all children's development. You may need to help a child with additional needs to play with their peers. They may find it physically difficult to access the activities, mix with others or struggle with social skills.

Early years practitioners can play a vital role in initiating early friendships.

You may need to think about

- Health and safety risk assessment
- Splitting the children into smaller groups
- Use of special equipment
- Physical access
- Changing the layout of the room
- Adapting toys e.g. using Velcro to anchor toys to a table (see Play Talks pack on **www.scope.org.uk**)

'Other children just see another child and accept her as she is. They don't have any hang-ups. Adults could learn a lot!'
Parent

'When each person is valued for who they are and differences are appreciated everyone feels included and understood whatever their personality, abilities, ethnic background or culture.'

EYFS

It is worth researching the 'circle of friends' approach which enhances inclusion in a mainstream setting. It works by using the young person's peers to provide support and engage in problem solving with the person in difficulty. Try **www.inclusive-solutions.com/circlesoffriends.asp**

Being different – fitting in

Try to put yourself in the child's shoes. Some children may be oblivious that they are different or act differently to other children while others are acutely aware.

Some may rise to the challenge of an early years setting with ease. Others may become quite shy and be overwhelmed.

We all experience a wide range of feelings. Children slowly learn to manage their emotions with the help of adults.

Some children may find certain situations very difficult and may present challenging behaviours. Children with communication difficulties may present poor social skills and high frustration levels. For example, the room may be too noisy at times or there may be too many children in the room. A child may be tactile defensive i.e. not liking to be touched, particularly on their left side and not like anyone near that side.

Tips

- Understand the child's specific needs
- Ask parents for suggested solutions to any issue
- Seek advice from SENCO or other professionals working with the child

Invisible children – creating a disabled-friendly environment

Take a good look at your setting, your facilities, your toys, etc. In just the same way that you need to reassure parents that all children are welcome, youngsters need to feel confident and included.

For example:

A dinner trolley menu could show a photograph of spaghetti bolognaise, the words 'spaghetti bolognaise', the Makaton sign, the British Sign Language image and communication symbols for it.

Quite often children with disabilities are invisible in our society. Imagine being a child with additional needs but never seeing an image or a toy of a child with a similar impairment. They may feel left out, different and not included. It can affect their self-esteem and confidence.

Does your setting:

- reflect images of different disabilities? look at your wall displays – what do they show?
- reflect the idea that all children are welcome?
- include examples of different communication systems?
- have toys with hearing aids, glasses, leg or arm splints, diabetic wrist bands, tube fed dolls, teddies in wheelchairs, etc.?
- story books which include tales about children with additional needs?

Making early friendships is important for all children. If their child has a communication difficulty it may mean parents are unaware of any budding friendships.

Tips

- Encourage social get-togethers
  - Tell parents who their child is friendly with
  - Organise parent/child events, e.g. coffee mornings, teddy bears' picnics, etc.

Including everyone

Equality begins when we look at everything we offer all children and families and ask how inclusive is this?

It is important to plan ahead to ensure you include everyone. Look at your weekly timetable and identify possible challenges.

Tips

- Discuss with parents any particular issues – invite them into the setting
- Ask professionals how other settings have managed particular situations
- Discuss with other staff if they feel they need further training/advice to become more confident

Make sure you try to include everyone throughout the day. For example, if a child needs to be fed by a tube into his tummy at meal times he can still sit at the lunch table with the other children. Or if a child has a visual impairment make sure everyone introduces themselves when they come into the room. You could put a note on the door asking people to do this.

Tips for inclusion

- Every child needs to be given choices as appropriate
- Every child needs to have a turn to perform special tasks such as being drink monitor
- Every child needs to have a turn at going first at something
- Every child needs to learn to wait
- Every child needs to learn to share
- Every child needs to face achievable challenges
- Every child needs to build on their abilities and strengths; to promote their learning and enjoyment rather than focusing on difficulties

Healthy risk taking

Risk taking is necessary to see how far we have developed and how well we can cope.

Early years practitioners may want to shield a child with additional needs from taking risks. If a child has health problems that desire may be even stronger.

'When a disabled child wants to try to be more independent, try out a new game or pastime or go it alone, we may hedge their actions with safety precautions. Some of these safety precautions are about our fears for the child and some are about our fears for ourselves. We often assess risks as if we can rule them out completely and are unwilling to subject ourselves or the children to anything that might carry risk.'

'Games All Children Can Play' from Scope (www.scope,.org.uk)

Risk assessments need to be used sensitively and as a tool to encourage healthy risk taking rather than deny the child access to usual play activities.

There may be times when you need to adapt some play activities so everyone can take part.

Tips

- Does the child want to take part in the activity?
- If so, are there changes which can be put in place to minimise risk?
- Does your room need rearranging?
- Could the activity be floor-based instead of at a table where the child can't reach?
- Do all staff know of changes being made to minimise risk?

Therapy programmes

Some children may have specific therapy programmes which need to be carried out daily. These could include a Portage programme which is a home-visiting educational service for pre-school children with additional support needs and their families, or a speech and language programme.

With practical thinking and planning it should be easy to include these into everyday activities.

'My daughter had to use a stander every day. I was delighted to find her one day in her stand with a ring of children dancing round her. They were all holding pompoms and having a great time enjoying the music. My daughter was doing her physio but was included at the same time and loved being the centre of attention.' Parent

Tips

- Seek advice from parents
- Consult professional help – get a written programme for your setting to follow
- Invite parents and professionals into the setting to show how to follow the programme
- Consider whether a key worker should attend a clinic appointment with the parents?
- Look at staff training needs

However, there may be times when it is not safe or practical for a child to take part in a particular activity. Instead, the child could be put in charge of directing or controlling the activity. This could mean ringing a bell or pushing a buzzer to stop or start an activity,

Or during a game of 'Simon Says' they could help choose what actions the other children have to copy next.

'My daughter used to attend Brownies and they would play ladders – a game where all the girls sat in twos facing each other legs, outstretched to form a 'ladder'. Each pair was given a number and when it was called they had to run down the 'ladder' as fast as they could. My daughter uses a wheelchair so it was not practical or very safe for her to join in. So instead she called out the numbers and controlled the game.' Parent

Tips

- Seek advice from parents
- Consult the speech and language therapist for advice
- Invite a speech therapist to the setting to share advice or train staff
- Consider other staff training needs. They could learn to sign nursery rhymes using British Sign Language or Makaton and encourage the children to learn with them

All children are unique. We all have strengths and weaknesses. By seeing the child first and disability second, practitioners can gain the confidence to include all children.

Starting at an early years setting

Starting at an an early years setting is a big step for all children. It may be their first experience of time away from their parents and siblings. Children with additional needs must learn to stretch their boundaries too. Parents want their child to be welcomed and to be treated like any other child.

'Providers have a responsibility to ensure positive attitudes to diversity and difference – not only so that every child is included and not disadvantaged but also so that they learn from the earliest age to value diversity in others and grow up making a positive contribution to society.'

EYFS

Government guidance to early years settings clearly states that providers are expected to welcome all children and offer an inclusive atmosphere by:

- Removing or helping to overcome existing barriers for children

- Being alert to signs of needs and responding quickly involving other agencies if necessary

- Stretching and challenging all children

- Ensuring all children regardless of needs experience an enjoyable programme of learning and development

Anxious parents

All parents worry when their child starts pre-school. Parents of children with additional needs will find this worry is magnified greatly. They may feel over protective of their child especially if they have complex health needs.

Learning to trust relative strangers to look after their most precious child will take time. They need to feel listened to, respected, and treated as a partner who is valued for their knowledge and expertise about their child.

Parents want to feel confident that the setting can cope with their child's needs. They will seek reassurance about how you will deal with any issues and need to know of your experience of including children with additional needs.

But equally they may feel unable to ask key questions, and be frightened of making waves or putting up barriers as to why their child may not be included in the setting. They will not want to make practitioners anxious about coping with their child.

Some parents may still be coming to terms with their child's needs and may not yet be aware of any implications for starting an early years setting.

All children are unique and all children with additional needs are different from each other. It is not so much your experience of including all children that counts but rather a positive attitude and a welcoming atmosphere for everyone.

Staff cannot be expected to know everything but settings which demonstrate a willingness to learn, seek advice and develop good practice to help their children will offer vital reassurance to parents.

- Does your setting include a variety of images of disabilities on show?
- Do you have a selection of books which include characters with additional needs? (see **www.childreninthepicture.org.uk**)
- Do you have wheelchair dollies and teddies, tube-fed dolls, or a hearing aid or glasses, etc.? Choose carefully, these toys need to present a positive cheerful image

Planning ahead

The key to a smooth start into any setting is planning ahead. All staff need to feel confident and comfortable so that they can respond to the child's needs.

It is natural for staff to feel apprehensive but getting the right information and training early on should quell most concerns. Many charities provide advice, support and training on particular conditions (see Useful resources section).

It is important that staff don't get too bogged down in the additional or medical needs of the child but remember that there is a young person there too. That is not to say that additional needs are not important but staff need to see the child first and the disability second.

Tips

- Review your information form used to enroll a child at your setting:
  - Does it highlight the social aspects of all children?
  - Does it focus on what they can do and what they like to do, as well as where they need help?
  - An 'All about Me book' or Communication passport is a good way to get to know all children but this needs to be regularly reviewed as their needs/likes may change as the child settles into the setting.
  - Be flexible about settling in and visits to the setting. Some children may take longer to really settle in
  - Key worker/person needs to maintain regular contact with the family as the setting gets to know the child

Getting the right support

It is essential settings make sure key early years practitioners are fully informed with the right up-to-date information.

Settings also need to be aware that extra support is available to include children with additional needs under five through the Early Years Action and Early Years Action Plus schemes (see Moving on section). This can be organised through the local Special Educational Needs Co-ordinator (SENCO). The Early Support website **www.earlysupport.org.uk** has details about the scheme.

- Consider how you gather and record information
- Review early years practitioners knowledge. Do staff know who to contact for more information, support or training?
- Does the child's family already have an Early Support tool kit (**www.earlysupport.org.uk**) which could be used as a starting point?
- Do your homework – try not to make the parents repeat everything again and again
  - Seek parental permission to contact any professionals already involved with the family
  - Check the parents' understanding of what they may have been told
  - Clarify any concerns parents' may have and how they would like them addressed

It is important to work with parents and be honest if there are concerns or issues. Staff and parents need to be able to work together in a partnership.

Home visits

It can be very helpful for staff to visit a child and his parents at home. It is the best place to see the child relaxed and happy in their own environment.

If possible the visit should include the key person or contact for the family and child.

Some parents can find home visits daunting and even intrusive, especially if their child has recently been diagnosed and may have already had contact with a number of other professionals.

Many parents talk about the need to tidy up and get the vacuum out before any visit, creating more pressure and anxiety for them.

- Ask parents if they are happy to have a home visit or would they prefer to meet at the setting or another venue
- Try to put yourselves in their shoes. How would you feel about having relative strangers coming into your home at a particularly vulnerable time? It can feel overwhelming especially if they are nervous about their child starting pre-school
- Be patient – be aware of conflicting emotions that parents may be going through – letting go of their child even for a few hours a week is a huge step
- Where possible try to let parents suggest a good time for the visit to fit in with the demands of other family members, work commitments, hospital/clinic appointments, etc.
- Inform parents who will be attending the visit and the purpose of it
- Take along some toys from the setting for the child to play with and ask them to show you some of their own
- If parents agree invite other key professional(s) to the visit

At the end of the visit it is important that parents are clear what happens next, such as a visit to the setting, starting date, gradual integration into the setting, etc.

Make sure parents have the contact details of their key person in case of any queries. Ensure parents have a copy of all the information gathered.

Risk assessment

All early years settings need to carry out and manage risk assessments in order to include children with additional needs.

It is important that the child and other children are not exposed to unacceptable risks and that they can take part in all the activities. Similarly it is important staff can carry out activities safely and any risk to them is minimised. (See Unique child section.)

'Games All Children Can Play' from Scope **www.scope.org.uk** gives practical ideas to include all children safely.

'The Dignity of Risk' from the Council for Disabled Children **www.ncb.org.uk/cdc** is aimed at professionals working with children with additional needs and their families. It concentrates on practical issues such as moving and handling, personal care and physical intervention and has practical forms and protocols.

Handle with Care is a practical guide and invaluable tool for all practitioners involved in moving and handling children and young people. It gives an insight to the issue from the child's point of view. Visit **www.sccyp.org.uk**

Health care plans

Children with complex health needs will need to have a health care plan which is individual to them. Look at 'Including Me – managing complex health needs in schools and early years settings' from the Council for Disabled Children (**www.ncb.org.uk/cdc**). This is a really useful handbook for all practitioners which contains lots of detailed illustrations of good practice and ready to use forms and letters to get settings started.

The health care plan needs to clarify what level of support a child will receive, who is responsible for particular activities and identify any training needs and training agencies.

The plan needs to be very detailed and cover a holistic approach to all the child's needs.

Tips

- Allow plenty of time and plan ahead to get a detailed health care plan written

Health care plans need to be drawn up by all key professionals involved with the child and their parents. They need to be dynamic and regularly updated according to any changes in the child's needs or condition.

For further information please refer to 'Managing Medicines in Schools and Early Years Settings' by the DfES/DH now DfCSF **www.standards.dfes.gov.uk/eyfs/resources**

Special equipment

Some children with a physical impairment may need special seating, standing or walking frames.

Sometimes parents may be able to send in the equipment daily with the child but this may not always be practical or possible.

Early years practitioners need to consult with the relevant professionals (such as physiotherapist or occupational therapist) for advice about particular equipment which may be needed. Any equipment needs should be identified in the child's health care plan.

Staff may also need advice on how to use the equipment. In most cases this can be delivered by the parents. Invite them into the setting to train staff. This will not only empower the family and help build a stronger relationship with your setting but enable more staff to learn at the same time.

Often early years settings may have concerns over whether they have enough space to use the equipment and there may also be storage issues for when the equipment is not in use.

Funding applications can also be long and complicated and it is essential that any equipment needs are assessed as early as possible.

Toilet training can be a frustrating process; especially if the child has a learning disability. Mencap has produced a useful practical guide (see **www.mencap.org.uk**). For some children with physical difficulties you may need advice from an occupational therapist and/or a continence service nurse.

Tips

- Plan early – check on any key equipment needs the child may have
- Try to incorporate any therapy or equipment into play activities, for instance, water play can be enjoyed in a stander or a specialist seat. This makes the child feel more included and any differences to other children are diminished

Some children may arrive wearing special splints on their bodies, hands, arms or legs, or special shoes and boots. All staff working with the child need to be aware of how to remove and put on the splints or shoes as well as any special wearing regime.

Consider these case studies:

Sarah has a learning difficulty and also has to wear supportive boots. She needs to wear them while standing and walking but is still getting used to them.
Discuss a suitable regime with the family and physiotherapist, e.g. Sarah could be allowed to take her boots off at circle and story time.

Thomas has epilepsy which is not under control and he needs to wear a helmet at all times in case he has a fit and falls over.

Jasmine has just started to wear a body suit and is still getting used to it. She needs to be praised and rewarded as well as distracted when finding it difficult.

Visits and settling in

Visits to the setting

Encourage both parents, where possible, to visit the setting with their child.

Some settings prefer to gradually integrate new children and encourage mum or dad to stay with the child on the first few occasions. This can be reassuring for all concerned, the early years practitioners, the parents and the child.

Some parents may be concerned about how parents of other children might react to their child's needs. Reassure them and encourage social opportunities to meet other parents. Some parents may find mixing with other families troubling at first and it is important that they are given support. It can be difficult to see other children developing and achieving milestones when your child is not.

It takes time for parents to adjust to explaining their child's needs to family, friends and anyone else they meet. Many parents can feel lonely and isolated. Sharing social experiences is vital for the parents and the children.

- Hold social events for parents to meet other families:
  - Coffee mornings
  - 'Stay and play' days
  - Teddy bears' picnics
- Tell parents who their child is making friends with to encourage play dates
- Encourage parents to talk about their child as a person not a child with a disability
- Encourage parents to attend any events - they may be reluctant at first and not feel up to it. Ensure their key person is available to offer support to the family at any social gathering
- Remember to find out about the parents' skills – they may be excellent organisers or have other hidden talents and in time could even help set up events

Settling in

Different children settle into new settings at different paces. It is essential you have good communication strategies with parents. (see Effective communication section.)

Tips

- Review how you share information about the child to parents
- Use a home/pre-school book – what would parents like to know? This obviously needs to be practical for the setting too
- Try to ensure that the key person has a regular (daily if possible) brief chat to parents
- Ensure parents know who to talk to if they have any concerns
- Make sure parents have somewhere private to talk
- Hold regular reviews with the family
- Work with parents to help make a Communication passport or 'All about me' book.
- Discuss any concerns openly and honestly. Try to deal with any issues as they occur. (See the Bumpy times.)

Positive thinking

Share positive achievements with the family – however small. It might be that their child found a particular situation funny or loved getting covered in paint, it doesn't matter how trivial.

Parents of children with additional needs spend their lives talking to professionals about what their child can't do.

Retelling fun or seemingly innocuous details about their child and letting parents know they are happy and settled at the setting is invaluable.

Building positive relationships

The Early Years Foundation Stage stresses the importance of good working partnerships between parents and professionals.

But what makes a good partnership? It is important for practitioners to think about what you would expect from parents and what you would offer them in return.

Try to put yourself in the parents' shoes. How would you like to be treated? What would you expect from professionals involved with your child?

Initial responses to your involvement from families will differ widely. It can depend on many factors including:

- How parents receive the news that their child may have an additional need. It will have a powerful impact on them
- How they have been treated by professionals previously involved with the family
- Whether previous professionals have listened to and acted on their concerns
- Their understanding of the situation and the information they have been given about their child's additional needs
- Whether they feel in control of the situation or powerless
- The impact it has on the whole family such as reduced income if one parent is unable to work
- The reaction and support they receive from family and friends

Tips

- Meet the family with an open mind – don't make assumptions – no two families are the same nor will they react the same
- Do your homework about the family and the child – contact other professionals involved with them
- Don't ask parents to repeat information again and again
- Check the parents' understanding of their child's needs and what it means
- Ensure parents have all the information they may need
- Be knowledgeable about local support groups for parents of children with additional needs
- Be prepared for negative reaction from some parents – professionals need to be able to step back without taking offence and return later offering further support. Parents can feel angry, utterly powerless and bewildered and fearful of the future – it is important professionals don't take their reactions personally and are able to offer objective but empathetic support

Early years practitioners need to treat parents as they would any other professional colleague. That means treating them on an equal basis with the same professional courtesy you would anyone else.

'I get really frustrated when professionals turn up late to appointments or have not allocated enough time for a meeting. It is insulting, like my time is not valued or important.' Parent

- Be honest but kind
- Don't promise what you can't deliver
- Remember it's okay to say you don't know – but offer to find out more or find a person who could help
- Arrive at meetings on time – or call if unavoidably delayed
- Let them know as soon as possible if you cannot attend an appointment
- If you can't finish everything at the meeting make another appointment when the discussions can be continued
- Be aware of parents' frustrations at accessing services/equipment – professionals need to be honest about the limitations of services/funding and acknowledge any inadequacies

Getting to know the parents

Names are so important. Make a point of remembering them. You would not call a colleague by their title e.g. SENCO. Equally it is important that practitioners maintain a professional distance (see Bumpy times section).

Tips

- Make a list of parents' names and use them regularly
- Ask them what they prefer to be called
- Remember sibling's names and ask after them too

So find out that Johnny's mum's name is Davinder Patel but she prefers to be called Vinny, not mum or Johnny's mum or Mrs Patel.

The EYFS states that families need to have a key person who is their main point of contact at your setting. That professional needs to:

- Introduce herself to parents in the way she wishes to be addressed

- Make sure they have her contact details

- Let them know if there is a better method of getting hold of her, such as phone, email, text, etc.

- Let them know the best times to catch her

- Let them know who to speak to if she is not available

- Have a home-setting agreement which sets out good practice and expectations from the settings, parent's and child's perspectives. Including Me – managing complex health needs in schools and early years settings and Working with Parents of Children with Special Educational Needs both have good practical examples of forms. (see Useful resources section for details)

- Not just ask about the child – ask how the parent is and mean it!

'My daughter was over 2 before anyone bothered to ask how I was. I was so flabbergasted I didn't know what to say.'   *Parent*

Respect

Different children settle into new settings at different paces. It is essential you have good communication strategies with parents. (see Effective communication section.)

The key basis of any good relationship is mutual respect. That is to say this needs to be a constructive two-way process.

Many parents do not always feel that they are treated with respect by some professionals. Similarly some professionals say parents do not always respect them for their views and expertise.

It is a question of building up trust on both sides. Parents will have many demands and issues to deal with. It is vital that early years practitioners are able to take a step back and look at things from the parents' point of view.

More assertive parents can be labeled troublemakers or 'pushy' for asking for information about their child's condition, his needs and how agencies are planning to support him. Yet professionals think nothing of bombarding parents for information time and time again. They expect parents to keep on providing the same details at the click of their fingers when this information may well be already available.

Think through why a parent appears to be so assertive? They need information and support so that they can feel empowered and get the best for their child.

They are not pestering you just to be difficult or cause trouble. They want to know how their child can best be helped, what resources are available and if and when they can have them.

Equally, professionals may appear to be demanding and assertive to parents. Having a constant stream of professionals asking them the same questions is not only draining, it doesn't raise parents' confidence. They can feel put upon. Parents want a partnership with practitioners who work with them and each other in a professional manner and keep themselves informed about the child and family's needs.

This should include information about services and equipment available as often parents do not know what to ask for.

'Often professionals ask you 'What do you want?'. Often we don't know because you can't ask for something which you don't know about.'   *Parent*

Tips

- Get information as early as possible – planning ahead is vital (see Starting at an early ears setting)
- Always avoid the use of jargon
- Don't do all the talking – let parents get a word in
- Answer questions in a precise way
- Be aware of the impact of what you say and how you say it. This can have a lasting impact on families (See Effective communication)
- How would parents like to receive information - letter, verbal reports, phone, or email?

Family dynamics

To really work effectively with parents practitioners need to understand the family dynamics. Families come in all shapes and sizes. Some may have stepfathers or stepmothers involved too. Some families have an extended network of support from grandparents, aunts and uncles, etc. Others may have fewer family members.

Don't forget dads too!

Parents of children with additional needs are subject to high rates of stress and are more likely to separate or divorce. (Department for Work and Pensions (DWP) and the Office for Disability Issues research into experiences of disabled people in rates of family formation, break up, re-partnering and having children, 2008)

Couples who stay together may have very different family roles. Often it is mum who takes on the child caring role and becomes the key family member who liaises with the professionals. Dad may be away at work and feel excluded from consultations about their child's needs and support.

It can be difficult for some dads to feel involved with their child, yet they have a vital role to play. Try not to make assumptions – all families are different and will react differently.

Tips

- Understand the family dynamics
- Find out how each parent is involved
- Look at your review practices – if a dad is working and cannot attend meetings find ways to ensure that he can get the information and has a chance to comment. This could be a follow up phone call or email.
- Is it possible to do a home visit at a time when both parents are available?
- If the parents are separated, discuss how dads can be involved in meetings too
- Where appropriate, stepfathers (and stepmothers) need to be involved too
- Look at ways to involve dads in your setting
- Encourage dads to link up with your setting, e.g. hold a fun event on a Saturday such as a play day for dads
- Be aware of any local father support groups
- Ensure cultural and language difficulties are taken into account

Siblings

The role of siblings within each family dynamic is vital. It is important to be aware of any issues affecting them which may be impacting on home life for everyone.

For example, some siblings can be badly affected through not getting enough sleep if their brother or sister tends to cry a lot. This can have serious knock on effects for the whole family.

Tips

- Remember the sibling's name and always make a point of saying hello if you meet them
- Let siblings be involved as much as possible
- Be aware of any local sibling/young carers groups

Parents are busy people too!

It is important to respect parents' time. It is as valuable as yours. Early years professionals have busy hard working schedules – but so do parents of children with additional needs, and it is no nine to five job.

There is no holiday or break for parents – it is 24 hours a day, 365 days a year and a life-long commitment.

Parents often have little quality time for themselves or each other. Even if their child is at pre-school few parents will be at home with their feet up. Chances to enjoy a coffee morning or a trip round the shops are rare.

It is highly likely that parents will be contacting a list of professionals to organise support, meetings or equipment while their child is absent. This is often the only time they can get hold of certain professionals during working hours

'In the beginning my life was one long round of appointments and clinics. On average I had two mornings a month when there wasn't something on – I didn't know what to do with myself!'
Parent

Tips

- Give plenty of notice of any events/review meetings – parents lives are often packed with meetings and clinic appointments
- Consider whether you really need the meeting?
- Try to keep all meetings friendly but focused
- Keep to time
- Inform parents of children with additional needs of planned changes in routines or visits outside pre-school
- Careful planning for change is vital for some children particularly those with an autism spectrum disorder. Parents and practitioners need to work together
- Consider setting up an email network of professionals involved with the family. Many parents find using emails a good use of their time as they can be sent any hour of the day or night to suit them

'I used to find it so frustrating as some clinics are only open on certain days of the week for set hours. Even if I was in at that time to make the call I would struggle to get through as the phone was always so busy.'
Parent

Remember parents bring their own skills and experiences with them. It can sometimes be forgotten that they are people too, as well as having a child with an additional need.

Somehow parents are expected to turn up to countless meetings, while coping with other family demands, work or study commitments.

'I was one of only three parents at my child's special school who worked. School were horrified when I said I couldn't come in the next day (about a non urgent matter) due to work commitments. They expected me to be available at their beck and call.'

Parent

Endless appointments

Some professionals need to be more aware of how much time and effort parents make in attending appointments only to be given the standard five minute slot. It is not just the time it takes but there may be costs involved to attend meetings such as having to take time off work.

Tips

- Always carry out what you have promised to do
- If you haven't had time to do something or there is a delay let the parents know and reassure them that you are still finding out what they need
- Review how you communicate with parents (see Effective communication)
- Get regular feedback from parents on how you are doing
- Try to remain friendly but focused

Record keeping

It can be very helpful for parents to contribute to record keeping of their child's progress. Parents will notice the smallest of changes. Look at developmental journals on the Early Support website (**www.earlysupport.org.uk**) which help families track, record and celebrate their child's achievements in the early years.

Tips

- Involve parents in record keeping
- Share and review record keeping together
- Discuss together ways to move the child forward
- Consult and encourage parents to help review policy
- Get to know the parents hobbies and interests – they may have a set of skills which could be invaluable to your setting
- Encourage parents to help at the setting perhaps in a volunteer capacity
- Invite parents to come into the setting with their child
- Use the parents' knowledge and expertise to contribute to training events for staff

Confidentiality

It is important to maintain dignity and confidentiality at all times. Settings need to have a private room for chatting and meetings.

Children's records must be kept securely. You should also consider who needs to be fully informed and have access to the child's records, that is who really needs to know.

For example there may be a child who has an egg or nut allergy. It is vital that all professionals concerned with the child are aware of that fact. But before sharing the news with other parents and children the setting must get permission from the parents first.

Tips

- Review what records you keep of the child and where you store them
- Look at who should have access to the records
- All children have a right to have their health details kept confidential

Working with other professionals

It is important that you are honest with yourself when as a professional you need to seek outside help. You need to inform parents who you would like to consult with and referrals to other agencies should be written sensitively.

For example, you may need to seek medical advice and support about a child's condition, how it affects them, details of medication and any therapies to be carried out.

This information will be sought from a wide variety of professionals including GPs, paediatricians health, visitors, etc.

Children with medical needs will need a health care plan put in place and this will need to be regularly reviewed. (See Starting at an early years setting.)

Gathering all necessary information can take time especially if there is a large number of professionals involved.

Tips

- Plan well ahead
- Be realistic about what can be achieved

Professional boundaries

It is important practitioners do not become over friendly with parents. There is a fine line to tread to ensure that you are friendly and supportive without creating a too close bond which may create problems or friction at a later date. (See Bumpy times section.)

Some parents may have limited opportunities for adult contact and conversation and could become reliant on some professionals. It is important that they have the chance to meet other parents in similar circumstances.

Encourage parents to talk about their situation. Many find it useful to meet other parents in similar circumstances.

Tips

- Don't become embroiled in personal issues with a family
- Don't gossip about families with other parents
- Never promise what you can't follow through
- Be honest and say if you need more time to get information
- Rearrange meetings if you need more time to prepare – you will be more productive in the long run
- Keep informed about local parent support groups such as Face2Face schemes **www.face2facenetwork.org.uk** where parents of children with additional needs befriend other parents. Every local education authority will also have a parent partnership scheme which can offer practical support and advice to parents of children with additional needs

Establishing good working partnerships with families can ensure real practical support for them which is invaluable. Respect their views, the pressure they are under, their time constraints and value their experience. Above all treat them as you would like to be treated.

Bumpy times

It is important to be aware of the rollercoaster ride that parents of children with additional needs may be on.

Parents are carried along the fairground ride at different speeds. Some may even travel backwards for a time or get stuck in one position.

Many professionals seem puzzled when a mum who was 'fine' last week doesn't seem the same person a couple of days later. Many events can happen which can upset the apple cart, aside from the usual day-to-day pressure we all live with.

'I think it is very easy for professionals to forget we still have all the usual every day issues to deal with on top of everything for our child(ren). We still have bills to pay, cars to be taxed, washing machines which need fixing, etc. It can be hard to find the time to fit everything in.'
Parent

There are many occasions when parents may feel extra stressed and anxious. An effective early years practitioner will support parents through these times and can help motivate them to take control of their situation.

'Thanks to a brilliant childminder I was able to keep working even at the most stressful times. I was able to get a break and had someone to share all the highs and lows with – it was invaluable.'
Parent

Under pressure

Many parents never quite get over the feelings of guilt and drown in a sea of appointments which can seem to achieve very little except create more frustrations and endless battles to get services, equipment and funding.

Frustration levels may run especially high if families are fighting to arrange or waiting for appointments, or trying to get funding for key bits of equipment.

Parents can become scarred and battle weary or cynical and appear to switch off. This can happen at different times for different people. It is a coping mechanism when parents feel that they can't handle any more pressure.

This pressure parents feel under cannot be emphasised enough. It is like a pressure cooker which will have to let off steam at some point.

'We just struggle on day after day. It is impossible to make plans and do normal ordinary things.'
Parent

This in turn puts tremendous strain on parents and their relationships. Research has shown a higher proportion of marriages or partnerships fail as a result of the pressures they feel under.

Parents feel they are always being judged. They have to reveal very personal and intimate details about family life in order to receive benefits, respite care and funding for equipment.

They may be asked to do something that they don't feel confident about or may struggle with feelings of being out of their depth.

They may fail to feel like a mum or dad but more like a carer with very few fun times.

'When I was pregnant I was a young carefree 24-year-old looking forward to being a mum. When my daughter was born I was suddenly expected to be able to inject her with Valium to stop her seizures. It was a nightmare.'
Parent

'I am often asked – 'how do you cope?' The simple answer is I often don't feel like I am. You just plod on and take a day at a time.'
                                                                                                    Parent

Tips

- Be aware of how many professionals the family have to deal with
- Be aware of any key appointments
- Find out what parents are hoping to achieve from the appointment
- If possible help parents prepare questions for the appointment
- Always ask how the appointment went
- Check what information the family received
- Action any key points which may affect your setting

Diagnosis

Receiving a diagnosis for their child is an emotional time for everyone. For some parents who have been convinced that something is wrong, this can be a welcome release that someone is finally listening to them.

For others it may come as a complete shock. Early years practitioners can support parents to come to terms with the situation and look at what help and support their child might need both now and in the future.

Tips

- Go at parent's pace – allow time for diagnosis to sink in
- Clarify their understanding
- Don't bombard them with questions and ask them to make decisions until they are ready
- Ask parents to come in or visit them at home, if they prefer, to discuss how the child can be best supported
- Don't assume how the parents are feeling – we all react differently
- Do some research on the child's syndrome or condition
- Get advice from appropriate professionals
- Find out about support groups/charities who can help
- Meet regularly and remember parents will need ongoing support
- Respect confidentiality and share information on a need-to-know basis

Children with no diagnosis

Many children with additional needs do not have an official diagnosis. This can be problematic not only for parents to understand their child's needs but it can also be difficult when filling in forms for benefits .

Children can be labeled with 'developmental delay' and there may not be an obvious cause. Some children will never be given an official diagnosis and this can bring endless frustration for parents.

The term developmental delay can be misleading – after all delayed trains always get there in the end. It may be sometime before parents realise that their child may not achieve certain milestones. Having no name or syndrome means they can't research easily what the impact will be.

Numerous visits to clinics and hospital appointments can end in frustration as professionals are unable to answer parents' questions because they don't know the answers.

Some parents need a clear diagnosis – a name to describe their child's condition. They are left in limbo and it can be hard to come to terms with the situation when there are no answers and there is so much uncertainty as to what the future holds.

There are many families across Britain who are desperately searching for information to understand their child's needs. They need to feel empowered. If they don't have a diagnosis it can be difficult to get the right support and services.

Some families will receive a diagnosis at a later stage but sadly some will never receive one. Finding other families in similar circumstances can support parents. The Face2Face organisation has a network of trained volunteer befrienders who can help parents make positive adjustments to the news that their child has a disability.
Visit **www.face2facenetwork.org.uk**

Early Support has produced a good booklet called When Your Child Has No Diagnosis **www.earlysupport.org.uk**. 'Contact a Family' has an excellent parent guide called Living Without a Diagnosis **www.caf.org.uk**

The charity Swan (Syndromes Without a Name) **www.undiagnosed.org.uk** supports families and promotes awareness of children who have undiagnosed disorders.

Tips

- Help parents to focus on the child not the disability
- Challenge yourself to see the child first not the disability – value the child, use their name not their condition
- Remember even for children with a diagnosis the future can still be very uncertain for parents. Having a label may not always help. No two children with the same condition will have the same abilities and needs. There can be vast differences. In time some parents learn to adjust to perhaps never knowing. But it can be very difficult as the first question parents are often asked is 'What's wrong with..?'

'When my daughter was six we were suddenly given a suggested diagnosis completely out of the blue. The diagnosis turned out to be wrong but it was like going through diagnosis all over again. It took me right back.'
Parent

Early years professionals need to be mindful to work with the parents at their own pace, reacting to their needs. No two families will be the same.

Tips

- Clarify the parents' understanding of their child's needs
- Find out details of local support groups
- Get information about charities which can help (see Useful resources)
- Be prepared to listen – having someone to talk to even if they don't have all the answers can relieve a lot pressure

Sometimes parents might receive some unexpected information which throws a spanner in the works. Parents need time and support to adjust to new situations.

'As a parent you might go into a meeting with an agenda of ABC. Then the consultant starts talking about XYZ and it can throw you. There can suddenly be a new set of issues we have to deal with that have come out of the blue and were completely unexpected.'
Parent

Listening to parents

Many parents know instinctively when something is not quite right with their child and may face a huge fight for their needs to be acknowledged.

This may be due to a rare condition or the child's symptoms not yet being apparent to the professionals concerned.

It is important that practitioners are always honest with families and clarify what issues parents are worried about.

Tips

- Really listen to parents concerns
- Discuss any issues with a key worker or SENCO
- Ask parents to contribute to record keeping
- Reassure parents about your own record keeping systems so they know you have a very accurate picture of their child in your setting

Telling others

Many parents find it difficult to explain to friends and family about their child's needs. They may also be fearful about the reaction from other children's parents at your setting and concerned that staff will now treat their child differently. Encourage parents to talk openly about their child, starting with trusted family members and friends.

Early years practitioners need to give reassurance to parents and focus on the child's strengths and how these will help any needs they might have.

Encourage parents to continue telling anecdotal stories about their child. Remember child first – disability second.

Tips

- Focus on what the child can do
- Tell parents who their child played with
- Encourage social get-togethers for children and parents

For example:

One mum of a boy with Downs syndrome organised a teddy bears' picnic for all the children her son would be mixing with at nursery. She encouraged parents to ask questions about her son's condition.

This was a brave parent, who at a very early stage, was able to discuss her son's needs with relative strangers. Some parents may never get to that stage but that is fine too.

Not all parents would feel able to take part in such an event. Early years practitioners need to encourage parents to talk about their child first and to be confident in explaining their additional needs. Generally the more they are able to talk about their child's needs the easier it becomes.

Showing support

Practitioners cannot always help parents with emotional issues but they can support and show interest in the child. This by itself can be invaluable – having someone else who gets to know their child and shares in their achievements however small is priceless. For example, all parents like to have something their child has made or painted to take home and be proud of.

It is really important parents receive positive feedback however small. If Johnny has managed to wait patiently for his drink that morning, make sure his parents know. It will give them comfort and encouragement.

'Even now that my child is fourteen I can probably count anything positive said about her by professionals on one hand. It's very sad.'
                                                                                                            Parent

Sometimes parents may feel overwhelmed if their child is not achieving the same things at home as in the early years setting or at the childminders. Parents may feel inadequate and not want their child to keep going to the setting.

Tips

- Emphasise the positives but offer reassurance to parents that all children react differently
- Acknowledge any difficulties the setting is finding and discuss how you plan to overcome them
- Encourage the parents to talk about positive things happening in the child's life at home
- Make sure the family has contact details for local support groups to offer emotional support or advice

Taking a break

There may be times when it is important for the family to take a break from any reviews, clinics and hospital appointments.

It is worth suggesting to some families that they plan set breaks each year when they don't attend any meetings but try to have as normal a life as possible.

This is easier said than done as parents can wait weeks or months for crucial hospital appointments.

Tips

- Encourage parents to block out certain weeks in their diary as family times
- If this is not possible try to ensure families have spells when they limit the amount of appointments they attend
- Make sure parents are happy with the time and date of any meetings you plan with them
- Give them the option of changing it
- Inform families of any short break services in your area, e.g. Home Start, Family Link, respite care centres or sessional workers

'I was horrified when a well meaning professional suggested we had a week off from appointments. In fact it was the best advice I could have had but I didn't feel I could say no I am not free that week.'
                                                                                                            Parent

Raising concerns

It is important that early years practitioners are able to raise any concerns with parents.

For example some parents may become over protective and find it hard to discipline their child with additional needs. Some may also permit inappropriate behaviour which they wouldn't allow siblings to get away with.

Try to focus on how you can work together to help their child rather than make the child's needs the issue.

It is important to keep an open dialogue with parents. A home and setting book can be a good communication tool. However the written word can sometimes be misinterpreted and nothing beats face-to-face contact.

Tips

- Try to raise concerns face-to-face or on the telephone
- Listen to the parents' point of view
- Try to work together – ask the parents for suggested solutions
- Honesty first and foremost
- Tackle any issues on the day they arise – don't let things fester
- Respect parents' wishes
- Always deal with any money or payment issues privately
- Be ready to back up any comments with practical examples
- Finish any difficult conversation on a genuine and positive note

Conflicting views

Professionals need to be prepared for periods when there will be conflicting views. This could be between the family and some professionals, or between professionals.

Parents want the best for their child, disability or not, and have a right to seek a second opinion.

Early years practitioners need to make sure they still respect the parents' views and remain nonjudgmental. They can do so by ensuring that they are putting the child's needs first and foremost.

Some parents may refuse to accept what they have been told. Practitioners need to be able to put a bad reaction behind them and come back with further support.

When a child is ill in hospital

Children with more complex needs may spend large amounts of time in hospital. It is of course a very worrying time for the whole family and has a huge impact on everyone.

It is important that early years practitioners maintain contact with the family and support them as much as possible.

Lengthy hospital stays can easily leave families feeling very isolated and cut off or out of the loop. It can be an exceptionally stressful time for all concerned as mum and dad may have to juggle work demands and make sure siblings' needs are met.

'We spent a lot of the early years in and out of hospital. It was amazing how quickly you became institutionalised and cut off from every day life.' *Parent*

If a hospital stay is planned and the parents are happy to reveal what is going to happen your setting can do a lot to help prepare the child, such as reading stories about going to hospital and having operations or playing doctors and nurses.

Tips

- Maintain confidentiality – seek parents' permission first before talking about hospital and doctor's visits
- Find out what information your local hospitals have for children and their families
- Contact the family once a week while in hospital – this could be by phone or email – whatever the parents prefer

- Send get well cards and pictures from their classmates – it lets parents know how important their child is and that they are missed
- Take photographs of what has been happening at your setting to share with the family
- If the child is to have continued medical needs they may need a health care plan put in place before they return. Including Me – managing complex health needs in school and early years settings from the Council for Disabled Children has excellent examples of how to write and implement health care plans
- Ensure parents receive all usual correspondence including newsletters

Life-limiting conditions

Some children have degenerative or life-limiting conditions where they may be losing skills over a period of time. This can be emotionally hard for everyone to deal with. Some children may be prone to chronic infections and/or may not be well enough to attend an early years setting very often. They may also miss out on many other social occasions.

The pressure on parents of these children will be enormous and many may find it hard to trust a setting to look after their child. The whole family will be under huge amounts of stress and strain including any siblings.

Parents will want to ensure their short lives are as fun-packed as possible. The child needs to be treated like any other.

Tips

- Remember child first, disability second
- Emphasise the positive small achievements – keep a photographic record to give to the family
- If a child is away from the setting for long periods make sure they are sent cards and pictures from their peers. Look at setting up webcam links so the child and family can stay in touch with the setting and their friends
- Children with health needs will need to have a health care plan which identifies the level of support a child needs in any setting and who is responsible for a particular task. This will need to be regularly reviewed for children with a degenerative condition
- Risk assessments will need to be carried out and regularly reviewed
- Ensure there is good liaison with the local palliative care team to ensure support for the whole family. Providing good social support is essential
- Make a point of remembering sibling's names, ages, interests and speak to them whenever you see them
- Provide information and support or refer to specialist services. The Association of Children's Palliative Care charity has a useful website - **www.act.org.uk** Contact A Family – **www.caf.org.uk** can also put parents in touch with others who have children with similar conditions
- Ensure good joined-up working between all agencies involved, putting the family's needs at the centre
- Review supervision support services for staff involved with the family

Knowing your boundaries

Working closely with families who have children with additional needs can be one of the most important and rewarding roles for early years practitioners.

Having a good bond between parents and professionals is so important. Supporting families through difficult times can help seal that bond.

How involved practitioners become is a personal choice but it is important they in turn have the right support.

Practitioners need to have regular review meetings with their manager, key worker or area SENCO to exchange information and discuss any issues which have arisen.

Tips

- Treat parents as you would any other professionals
- Don't make promises you can't keep
- Let parents know if there has been an unavoidable delay
- Share information on a need-to-know basis only
- Don't become over involved in personal family matters

Pushy parents

This is often a term given by professionals to parents who are seen to be a nuisance and who pester them for information or services.

Some parents cope with their situation by empowering themselves. They need to be pro-active to help their children and are keen to find out all they can and to get all the equipment and services they need.

Professionals need to remember that they in turn bombard parents for information and expect them to provide it at a drop of a hat.

There needs to be mutual respect on both sides. Parents have a right to know what help is available for them and professionals need to acknowledge that parents are the experts when it comes to their child.

Above all professionals need to remember that these parents are first and foremost simply parents who want the best for their son or daughter.

Effective communication

Good communication between families and professionals is the key to a successful and effective partnership.

Communication is a two-way process, an exchange of information. Early years practitioners need to remember to really listen as much as they inform.

Building common ground

Building up trust on both sides is vital in order to establish respect for parents and early years practitioners. Respect has to be earned and is not an automatic right. It may take time for parents to adapt and trust practitioners. They may be feeling very vulnerable and have a lot to take on board.

Early years practitioners who pay attention to the small details will build up trust far quicker. Taking time to chat for an extra minute can pay dividends at a later date. Establishing a good rapport early on can make any possible contentious issues which might arise easier to handle for all concerned.

'Having to raise a sticky issue with a professional you have good communication with is a lot easier than those you find hard to talk with and don't feel there is any rapport.'   *Parent*

It can be difficult for some professionals to view parents on an equal basis. Indeed the term 'professionals' seem to suggest they are the experts.

But an insightful practitioner will always remember that parents are the real experts about their child and will always demonstrate this in everything they do. Parents will notice the slightest and smallest changes in their child.

All too often parents don't have any outlet to share the small steps of progress their child makes. Their friends will be chatting about how their children have achieved the usual developmental milestones, be it learning to sit/walk/run/use the potty, etc. To a parent of a child with additional needs this can seem a long way off or even unachievable.

Having someone to share and enthuse with them and celebrate progress however small is invaluable.

It can be difficult for parents of children with additional needs to share their child's success, such as 'my child held her head up for 10 seconds today'. Friends with able-bodied children may fail to understand the huge significance of such a statement and how much such a tiny step can mean. Even truly close friends who have children with no additional needs may fail to understand.

'I remember being so thrilled the first time my daughter picked up a spoon that I rushed round to tell a very supportive friend (who had two able-bodied boys). I remember seeing the slight puzzlement on her face as to why I was so excited. Being able to pick up a spoon was something so ordinary to her she didn't understand what a ground breaking moment it was.'   *Parent*

Yet early years professionals are in an ideal situation to share these small but momentous joys.

Making time

Parents may often feel rather like an object on a conveyor belt stopping off to see numerous professionals who will rarely bother to get to know them as people. They become 'Fiona's mum' or worse still, the 'Downs boy's mum'.

Few professionals will make the time to ask the parents their name or what they do for a living and will automatically call them mum or dad.

Sadly too often parents get used to being talked at rather than listened to. It can be hard for time-pressed professionals to find the time needed for parents.

'You can wait months for an appointment and then only get a few minutes with the professional to find there is no time to ask questions or they are just ignored.'   *Parent*

But paying attention to the simple things like getting names and titles right really matters and can make such a difference. Make an effort to talk about everyday matters even if only briefly. Find out about any siblings in the family, their ages and what they like to do.

Being a parent of a child with additional needs can be a very lonely role even though they may meet numerous people every day. It can be very easy for parents to become cut off and to feel out of the loop. They may not have the time or energy (especially if their child doesn't sleep well) to see old friends and have the opportunity to chat about the latest soap, gossip, news or to share a good joke.

Often the only adults parents may come into contact with will be the professionals involved with their child. This is especially true for children with complex health needs who may have twenty five plus professionals involved.

'Sometimes it can be a relief when a professional will chat about everyday things. It makes a change from always focusing on disability issues. It makes me feel more 'normal'.   *Parent*

It should also be remembered that most of the professionals involved in the parents' life are only there because of a child's additional needs.

Early years practitioners have the perfect opportunity to really get to know the child and celebrate with the parents their achievements, however small, and enjoy their personality traits.

Being able to chat easily about everyday things really helps to break down barriers and makes it easier to broach any serious issues which may arise.

Honesty first and foremost

Any trust built up between parents and practitioners can be lost very quickly if people are not honest. Early years practitioners may find it difficult to answer some questions honestly. But without honesty what happens to any communication? It breaks down and any gap between home and setting can be hard to repair.

Similarly it is important that early years practitioners acknowledge when they don't know the answer to parents' questions. We can't all be 'experts' in everything.

Tips

- Don't be afraid to say 'I don't know'
- Offer to contact someone who could answer the question
- Follow through with what you promised
- Contact parents if there has been an unavoidable delay

Highs and lows

Remember that parents live with what can seem a bewildering situation 24/7, 365 days a year. They don't go home at the end of the day and switch off.

Professionals need to remember that parents continue to sit on a rollercoaster ride with extreme highs and lows.

Just because the parents seemed fine the last time you spoke to them, it doesn't mean they will be like that next time.

There could a multitude of reasons which can affect parents' behaviour.

How they are treated by other professionals will have a knock on effect with your relationship. If they haven't been listened to previously or got the services or advice they feel they need, this can make parents very angry and belittled.

They spend hours of their precious time attending meetings and can emerge feeling totally confused and that the meeting may have achieved very little.

Similarly some parents spend many long frustrating hours fighting to get funding for pieces of equipment for their child. Sadly it is still not uncommon for pieces of equipment to take so long in arriving that the child has out grown them by the time they arrive.

Or it could be one of the many things in life which trouble us all, such as a sick child or pet, leaking pipes, broken down boiler, family illness or bereavement.

- Be aware of key events in family life and any siblings' needs
- Check how the child is eating and sleeping
- Make a note of important clinic appointments – and ask how they went
- Be mindful of key outstanding issues around the child such as equipment needs
- Understand any negative reaction from parents and be prepared to maintain support without prejudice or judgment
- Deal with difficult issues as and when they arise

Parents' reactions

Not all parents will feel comfortable communicating with your setting. This may be due to a variety of issues including cultural or family reasons or perhaps negative personal experiences of formal education or social services. Parents' reactions will vary and need to be respected.

Some parents may seem 'switched off' from being involved. This can be a common reaction when parents feel overwhelmed by their situation. They may not feel confident in parenting or feel they don't really understand their child's needs or condition.

It is the responsibility of early years practitioners to help parents value their child and see the person first and the disability second. All parents want their child to be popular and part of the crowd. Make sure they know who their child gets on well with at your setting.

Tips

- Ask open ended questions to encourage conversation and avoid yes/no answers
- Don't do all the talking – let parents get a word in – let them do most of the talking if they wish
- Encourage parents to tell stories about their child
- Inform parents of any friendships made and encourage get-togethers
- Ensure parents get regular feedback that is positive
- Be friendly but focused
- Don't become too embroiled in family issues
- Thank them for their time – it is just as important as yours!

Keep talking

Early years practitioners who keep trying to maintain contact with the family will help parents feel more empowered and respected.

Whatever happens it is important to keep communication channels open at all times.

- Always clarify parents' understanding
- Make sure parents know how and when to contact you
- Make sure they know who to speak to if you are not available
- Go at the parents' pace – support them as needed
- Ensure confidentiality at all times
- Ensure your setting has support in place for practitioners as it can be emotionally draining dealing with families. In your setting review supervision protocol to ensure professionals can debrief and discuss ways to receive and improve the support they give

Communicating with parents in a range of different ways

It is important your setting has a range of ways to communicate with parents to involve as many as possible. Consider if you need the services of interpreters to cascade information.

All messages should be communicated in plain simple language. Never use jargon or abbreviations.

Suggested ways to communicate could be:

- Regular newsletter – both printed and emailed
- A home and setting book
- Photographs
- A parents' notice board
- A comfortable private room to hold meetings/chats
- Parent events such as coffee mornings, picnic, fund raising, etc.
- Open nursery mornings for parents to stay and play

- Review the ways you communicate with parents
- Ask parents how they would like to maintain contact and how often
- Maintain up-to-date information about local support groups and facilities. Try to provide information in different ways. Some parents may work long shift patterns and want web based help which they can access at anytime, others will find written information more helpful, and some may want phone numbers to talk to local support groups

Making the most of meetings

Ensure parents have as much notice as possible for any important meetings and reviews.

- Review how you inform parents about meetings
- Discuss with parents what the meeting is for
- Look at timings, venues, who is attending, etc.

- Ensure parents know who everyone is at the meeting and what their role is
- End a meeting by summarising what has been discussed and any actions needed by whom and by when
- Make sure parents have a copy of minutes or action points
- Set a time for any follow up meeting

Setting the right environment

Review the environment where meetings are held. Look at the layout of the room. Make sure there are no barriers such as tables between you.

'I was once given a child's chair to sit on at the meeting when everyone else was in an adult chair! It was very degrading and I didn't feel part of the meeting at all.'   *Parent*

Tips

- Arrange the furniture in a circle or horseshoe if space allows
- Look at the room layout and chairs used
- Avoid having professionals sitting behind desks – these create an artificial barrier
- Where possible always use chairs of equal height so no one feels at a disadvantage
- Ensure no one has light or bright sunlight shining in their eyes
- Check the room is not too hot or cold for everyone
- Make sure there are no interruptions
- Turn off mobile phones
- Plan enough time for the meeting – don't keep checking your watch

Body language

The importance of body language should never be underestimated. It is one of the principle ways humans communicate with one another, consciously or otherwise.

Early years practitioners need to have a friendly approachable style and be careful not to be too quick to judge parents. Try to adopt an open posture (no crossed arms or legs) and ensure you make eye contact with everyone in the room.

Think about your eye contact. It should be natural not intimidating. Try to speak clearly, without mumbling and don't use any jargon. But above all be natural – be yourself.

It is important you take time to prepare for meetings with parents. Be clear what information you need from parents and ensure you have done your homework first.

Closed questions

These can be used when you require a simple yes or no. They are useful to clarify and finalise a situation or to seek acknowledgement.

Open questions

These are questions that require a fuller explanation. They can be used to encourage parents to chat and contribute to the meeting. For example 'What does Reece like to play with? How do you know when Susan is upset?'

- Maintain regular eye contact when speaking or listening to parents
- Use some open questions to encourage parents to talk – this will give them confidence and show them you respect their views
- Plan ahead - make a list of questions you need to ask before you meet parents
- Don't cut off or interrupt parents before they have finished speaking
- Repeat key points parents have made to show you have listened and understood
- Wait and listen – don't feel afraid of pauses
- Be approachable but not overly friendly
- Don't just talk to one parent or carer – make sure you include everyone

More about communication passports

'All about Me' books or communication passports are increasingly being used by early years practitioners.

They are a simple and practical guide to help people interact with a child who has trouble communicating. They contain personal information about the child's needs, likes and dislikes, etc.

They may need to include information about their medical condition but are NOT a replacement for the childhood red books used by health visitors. These are essential medical records of a child's key development, eg. weight, height, vaccinations, and so on. The passport is the child's personal identity and is owned by them, NOT the parents or professionals.

The passports are important because they value the child, give them a voice and helps others to understand them. They also give the child some control. Passports should give positive problem-solving solutions to help the child and not be a catalogue listing the child's additional needs. They can be very useful in helping new staff and other people to quickly understand the child's personal needs.

They can be used for any child or adult of any age. They should be reviewed at least once a year or every six months if the child is very young.

The passports should go everywhere with the child especially to other early years settings and of course when they attend any where for the first time, for example, starting school.

Anyone who knows the child well can help make them. But the most important thing is to involve the child, where possible, from the beginning, letting them choose what they want to be included. Perhaps the child could help to make the passport or choose or colour a picture for the front cover.

The passports can be any colour, size or shape. They can be as simple or complex as needed. Whatever the design, they should be attractive, colourful, accessible and positive, not jargon-ridden or confidential. They can be handwritten or typed.

Use different coloured paper, pens, pictures of the child, their friends and family, symbols, photographs or pictures of everyday objects. Cut up old catalogues or buy an inexpensive picture dictionary. You don't need access to a computer to make passports. Handwritten passports are just as effective.

For example:

Edward would only eat Thomas the Tank Engine pasta, so the labels from the tins are stuck in his communication passport on his 'what I like to eat' page.

Whatever is included in the passport it needs to be a positive illustration of the child.

Involving parents or carers

Involving parents in creating passports is essential and can be a good way to improve the bond between setting and home. They can also help parents see their child first and disability second. They can be a positive tool for parents who feel they are doing something which can really help their child.

Personal Communication Passports, Guidelines for Good Practice has lots of useful tips. Contact Sally Millar, Call Centre, University of Edinburgh, Paterson's Land, Holyrood Road, Edinburgh EH8 8AQ. 0131 651 6236. **www.callcentrescotland.org.uk**

Scope early years has produced different-sized communication passport templates which can be adjusted to a child's needs. They can be downloaded from the website **www.scope.org.uk/earlyyears/** or call 02920662405.

The Early Support site has lot of practical materials to help families **www.earlysupport.org.uk** Cerebra will make personal profiles similar to passports for parents. **www.cerebra.org.uk)** The National Children Bureau has useful communication information at **www.ncb.org.uk**

Taking time to build up trust and respect pays dividends for all concerned. Without good communication with parents, practitioners will never really understand and meet the needs of the child and their family.

Moving on

Starting school is a big step for all children. For parents of children with additional needs finding the right school can be emotionally draining and challenging.

They may have many questions: Will their child be accepted? Can the school meet their needs? Will they make friends? Can the staff deal with any medical concerns? Should they go for mainstream or a special school? Will they get transport to a specialist setting?

It can be a very anxious and confusing time, going through a statutory assessment process, dealing with professionals' reports on their child.

The list of questions is endless. Parents need regular reassurance and support at this time as it can be very daunting trying to unpick the statutory processes.

'We had just started to understand what different medical professional roles meant and then we had to learn our way round the education system. It was completely overwhelming.'

Parent

Most children with additional needs will be able to attend a mainstream school. The local educational authority will have an admissions guide on all the schools in your area. The local authority Parent Partnership will be able to give families key information and support.

Supporting parents as children start school

For some children who need extra help before the age of five there is a graduated scheme of support, known as Early Years Action and Early Years Action Support. This can be organised through the local Special Educational Needs Co-ordinator (SENCO).

The Early Support website **www.earlysupport.org.uk** has lots of details about the scheme. It also has lots of materials to prepare parents for moving their child into full time education.

The SEN Code of Practice details how support is provided for children with special educational needs. The code defines rights for parents and carers. There is also a parent's guide called Special Educational Needs (A guide for parents) from DfCSF publications.
Visit **www.inclusion.ngfl.gov.uk**

The website **www.goodschoolsguide.co.uk** also has useful tips about special education needs.

Statements

A small percentage of children who have received Early Years Action and Early Years Action Plus may receive a special education needs statutory assessment. (Education Act 1996, SEN and Disability Act 2001, SEN Code of Practice Nov. 2001)

Some children's needs are too complex to be met without extra resources from the local education authority. The LEA may decide to hold a statutory assessment and look at whether they need to draw up a statement of special educational needs. A statement cannot be drawn up without a proper multi-disciplinary statutory assessment.

Meeting the different professionals who are assessing their child, receiving their reports and then the final statement can be very harrowing for parents.

Sometimes there are issues over the amount of help, therapy support or equipment funding available which can put even more pressure on the parents.

Early years practitioners need to be very mindful of when parents are going through the statutory assessment process and the impact it can have on them.

'Seeing my daughter's needs and disabilities written down in black and white was horrendous. I just wasn't ready to read about them – they seemed to be talking about an object or a number not my little girl.'

Parent

Finding the right school

All children are unique and what is right for one child may not suit another.

General points parents may need to consider when looking for the right school include:

- Proximity of the school to home – will their child be mixing with their friends or local peer group?
- Suitable environment – is the building right for their child?
- Class sizes
- Staff/child ratios
- Who will be in their peer group?
- Experience of staff in teaching children with additional needs
- Staff attitude – is there a 'can do' ethos – will their child be welcomed?
- Look at the school's special educational needs policy

All schools are regularly inspected. Ask to see the latest Ofsted (Office for Standards in Education) inspection report

Tips

- Encourage parents to visit several different schools
- Encourage them to write out a list of questions or concerns which need to be addressed
- Help parents to update their child's Communication passport or 'All about Me' book ready for school (Hold 'make passport' mornings for parents and children)
- Ensure there is support for parents when they meet the Special Educational Needs Co-ordinator (SENCO) to discuss their child's needs
- Try not to overload parents at this time – rearrange any regular review meetings if necessary
- Make sure parents have details of a key person at the child's new school who they can contact with any queries or concerns

Practitioners have a vital role to play. They can be supportive without trying to influence the parents' decision by listening to their concerns and helping families think through all their options.

Useful resources

Aiming High for Disabled children: better support for families
Department for Education and Skills
ISBN 978-1-84532-262-5

Children with Complex and Continuing Health Needs – the experiences of children, families and care staff
Jaqui Hewitt-Taylor
Jessica Kingsley Publishers
ISBN 978 1 84310 502 2

Early Years Foundation Stage – Setting the Standards for learning development and care for children from birth to five
Department for Children, Schools and Families
ISBN 978-1-84775-128-7

Extending Inclusion – Access for disabled children and young people to extended school and children centres: a developmental manual
Philippa Stobbs
Council for Disabled Children
ISBN 978-1-905818-31-0

Growing Together, or Drifting Apart? – Children with disabilities and their parents' relationship
Fiona Glen
One Plus One
ISBN 978 1 874207 15 3

Handle with Care – moving and handling children and young people
Laura Paton
Scotland's Commissioner with Children and Young People
www.sccyp.org,uk

Including Me – Managing complex health needs in schools and early years settings
Jeanne Carlin
Council for Disabled Children, Department Education and Skills
ISBN 1-904787-60-6

The Dignity of Risk – A practical handbook for professionals working with disabled children and their families

National Children's Bureau
ISBN 1904787 22 3

Working with Parents of Children with Special Educational Needs

Chris Dukes and Maggie Smith

Hands on Guides
ISBN 1-4129-4521-9 / ISBN 978-1-4129-4522-6 (pbk)

Contacts

Afasic

Charity for children and young adults with communication impairments

Tel: 020 7490 9410

Helpline: 08453 55 55 77

Email: info@afasic.org.uk

Web: www.afasic.org.uk

ASLTIP (The Association of Speech and Language Therapists in Independent Practice)

Provides information about independent speech and language therapists.

Answerphone: 0870 241 3357

Email: asltip@awdry.demon.co.uk

Web: www.asltip.co.uk

The British Dyslexia Association

Campaigns and provides support to break down barriers and enable dyslexic people to reach their potential.

Tel: 0845 251 9003

Helpline: 0845 251 9002

Email: helpline@bdadyslexia.org.uk or admin@bdadyslexia.org.uk

Web: www.bdadyslexia.org.uk

BILD (British Institute of Learning Disabilities)

Provides information, publications, training and consultancy services for organisations and individuals.

Tel: 01562 723010

Email: enquiries@bild.org.uk

Web: www.bild.org.uk

Bobath Centre

A treatment and teaching centre, providing specialist care for children and adults referred nationally and internationally for assessment and treatment.

Tel: 020 8444 3355

Email: info@bobathlondon.co.uk

Web: www.bobath.org.uk

Capability Scotland - for people with cerebral palsy

One of the country's leading disability organisations working for a just Scotland. They work with children, adults and families living with disabilities to support them in their everyday lives.

Advice line: 0131 313 5510

Email: ascs@capability-scotland.org.uk

Web: www.capability-scotland.org.uk

Cerebra - for brain injured children and young people

Helps to improve the lives of children with brain related conditions through research, education and direct support.

Tel: 01267 244200

Web: www.cerebra.org.uk

Contact A Family

UK-wide charity which provides advice, information and support to the parents of all disabled children.

Helpline: 0808 808 3555

Email: info@cafamily.org.uk or helpline@cafamily.org.uk

Web: www.cafamily.org.uk

Council for Disabled Children

Works to influence national policy that impacts upon disabled children and children with special educational needs (SEN) and their families. Provides training, conference and consultancy.

Tel: 0207 843 6000

Web: www.ncb.org.uk

DLF (Disabled Living Foundation)

Gives practical, unbiased information and advice on disability equipment.

Helpline: 0845 130 9177

Textphone: 020 7432 8009

Email: advice@dlf.org.uk or info@dlf.org.uk

Web: www.dlf.org.uk

Dyspraxia Foundation

Committed to making the teaching and medical professions more aware of dyspraxia; and to spread understanding of how those who have the condition can be helped.

Helpline: 01462 454 986

Tel: 01462 455016

Email: dyspraxia@dyspraxiafoundation.org.uk

Web: www.dyspraxiafoundation.org.uk

Early Support

National Government programme which aims to achieve better co-ordinated, family focused services for young disabled children and their families for local authorities. hospitals and community-based health services across England. Provides lots of information and products

Web: www.earlysupport.org.uk

Epilepsy Action

Campaigns to improve epilepsy services and to raise awareness of the condition.

Helpline: 0808 800 5050

Email: helpline@epilepsy.org.uk

Web: www.epilepsy.org.uk

Face2Face (Scope) – Parent to Parent befriending

A network of trained volunteer befrienders who can help parents make positive adjustments to the news that their child has a disability.

Tel: 0844 800 9189

Email: face2facenetwork@scope.org.uk

Web: www.face2facenetwork.org.uk

Fledglings

Operates a free search and supply service for toys and aids to help parents, carers and childcare professionals.

Tel: 0845 458 1124

Fax: 0845 458 1125

Email: enquiries@fledglings.org.uk

Web: www.fledglings.org.uk

The Foundation for Conductive Education

Teaches children and adults with physical disabilities such as cerebral palsy how to overcome their movement difficulties.

Tel: 0121 449 1569

Email: info@conductive-education.org.uk

Web: www.conductive-education.org.uk

HemiHelp – for people with hemiplegia

Offers information and support to families where there is a child with hemiplegia.

Helpline: 0845 1232372

Email: support@hemihelp.org.uk

Web: www.hemihelp.org.uk

I Can

The national educational charity for special schools, nurseries and centres within local schools and provides training and information for parents, teachers and therapists.

Tel: 020 7843 2510

Web: www.ican.org.uk

Makaton Vocabulary Development Project (MVDP)

Helps people with learning difficulties to communicate through signs and symbols.

Tel: 01276 606760

Email: info@makaton.org

Web: www.makaton.org

Mencap

Works with people with a learning disability to change laws and services, challenge prejudice and directly support thousands of people to live their lives as they choose.

Tel: 020 7454 0454

Email: help@mencap.org.uk

Web: www.mencap.org.uk

National Autistic Society

Aims to provide individuals with autism and their families with help, support and services that they can access, trust and rely upon. The website includes information about autism and Asperger syndrome, the NAS and its services and activities.

Tel: 020 7833 2299

Email: nas@nas.org.uk

Web: www.nas.org.uk

National Portage Association

A home-visiting educational service for pre-school children with additional support needs and their families.

Tel: 01935 471641

Email: info@portage.org.uk

Web: www.portage.org.ukc

NSPCC - safeguarding children

Aims to protect children from cruelty, support vulnerable families, campaign for changes to the law and raise awareness about abuse.

Helpline: 0808 800 5000

Email: help@nspcc.org.uk

Web: www.nspcc.org.uk

RCSALT (Royal College of Speech & Language Therapists)

The professional body for speech and language therapists and support workers.

Main Switchboard: 020 7378 1200

General Info: 020 7378 3012

Email: info@rcslt.org

Web: www.rcslt.org.uk

RNIB (Royal National Institute for the Blind)

RNIB offers information, support and advice to people with sight problems.

Tel: 020 7388 1266

Helpline: 0845 766 9999

Email: helpline@rnib.org.uk

Web: www.rnib.org.uk

RNID (Royal National Institute for Deaf People)

Aims to achieve a radically better quality of life for deaf and hard of hearing people.

Tel: 020 7296 8000

Information helpline: 0808 808 0123 (freephone)

Textphone: 0808 808 9000

Email: informationline@rnid.org.uk

Web: www.rnid.org.uk

Scope – about cerebral palsy - equality for disabled people

A disability organisation whose focus is people with cerebral palsy. Its aim is that disabled people achieve equality in a society in which they are as valued and have the same human and civil rights as everyone else.

Response helpline: 0808 800 3333

Email: response@scope.org.uk

Web: www.scope.org.uk

Sense - for people with multiple sensory impairments

An organisation for people who are deaf/blind or have associated disabilities.

Tel: 0845 127 0060

Textphone: 0845 127 0062

Email: info@sense.org.uk

Web: www.sense.org.uk

Syndromes Without A Name (Swan)

Helps raise awareness of children who suffer from undiagnosed disorders and aims to help families of sufferers by providing information and support.

Tel & Fax: 01922 701234

Web: www.undiagnosed.org.uk

Whizz-Kidz

Provides disabled children with mobility equipment, training, advice and support.

Tel: 020 7233 6600

Web: www.whizz-kidz.org.uk

Other titles in this series

Including Children with:

**Down's Syndrome
by Clare Beswick**

9781904187905

**Asperger's Syndrome
by Clare Beswick**

9781905019113

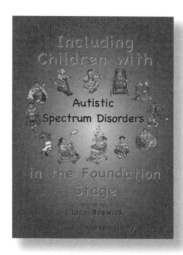

**Autistic Spectrum
Disorders (ASD)
by Clare Beswick**

9781904187288

**Attention and
Behaviour
Difficulties (ABD)
by Maureen Garner**

9781905019014

**Working Within
the P Levels
by Kay Holman and
Janet Beckett**

9781905019380

**Developmental
Co-ordination
Disorder (Dyspraxia)
by Sharon Drew**

9781905019458

All available from www.acblack.com/featherstone